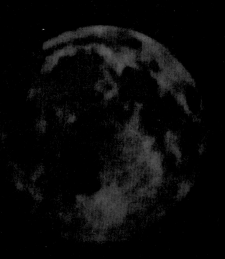

STUDIES
OF LIGHT

In the World and
on the Stage

JOSEPH P. OSHRY

Designed Lighting, LLC

Published by Joseph P. Oshry | Designed Lighting LLC
Copyright © 2021 Joseph P. Oshry | Designed Lighting LLC

ISBN 978-1-7343881-0-7
eBook ISBN 978-1-7343881-1-4

Library of Congress Control Number: 2020918173

For images of Rosco Gobos shown: All intellectual property rights in Rosco's Gobos including trademarks and copyrights in the gobos are owned by and used with permission of Rosco Laboratories, Inc.

All photos by the author unless otherwise noted.
Cover photo: *Miss Saigon*, Manatee Performing Arts Center, Bradenton, FL, August 2014
Title page photo: *A Little Night Music*, Manatee Performing Arts Center, Bradenton, FL, October 2017

Principal editor: Laurie Rosin; Concept Editor: Kim Northrop

Book design: Ron Toelke | www.toelkeassociates.com

DEDICATION

This book is dedicated to everyone who works with light as well as to those who want a greater understanding of how it can impact their life. Whether you are an experienced lighting designer or a homeowner who wishes to improve their environment, this book has something for you.

Throughout the four decades I've spent working with this medium, I've had the good fortune to meet many people who have taken an active interest in how light works. To all of you, this book is my way of saying thank you for your participation and interest.

This book is also dedicated to the memory of my brother, Michael A. Oshry — March 25, 1955 to October 28, 2020.

Fireworks (Photo courtesy of Amy Oshry)

Gaspar Ballet, Straz Center, Ferguson Hall, Tampa, FL, January 2012

CONTENTS

Alma Mater (Photo courtesy of Illinois State University)

FOREWORD

It's so much darker when a light goes out than it would have been if it had never shone.

—John Steinbeck, *The Winter of Our Discontent*

As a university professor, I enjoy special satisfaction when I encounter resounding echoes of the principles and practices that are the core of my instruction. This volume reflects and illustrates those principles and design practices.

Joe Oshry was a student in my lighting design courses. He showed considerable promise at that time, and his successful career as a lighting designer is no surprise. His work is special in that he has made those fundamental principles and practices his own and articulates them in his design work and thus this book.

Training the eye to notice, see clearly, and then document light is at the heart of designing a living light. How does the light originate at the source? How does the light get into the space? How does the light shape the space? How does light reflect from surfaces? How do the objects in the space absorb the light? How do we perceive color as revealed by absorbed and reflected light? The answers are imperative to managing light in all areas of design and in our lives.

I am honored to recommend the visual journey that awaits you. You will appreciate light anew as it is illustrated here. This volume entreats us to see and enjoy the qualities of light and realize how we respond to the properties of light. To do so with a renewed awakening can bring new meaning to the perception of our existence.

J. William Ruyle
Professor of Design, Emeritus
School of Theatre, Illinois State University, Normal, Illinois
September 25, 2020

Grand Central Station, New York City

Madama Butterfly, Opera Tampa, Straz Center, Carol Morsani Hall, Tampa, FL, November 2004 (Photo courtesy of Opera Tampa/Straz Center)

INTRODUCTION

A day without light is, well, night. — George Oshry 1945–2016

This book began as a series of images I periodically posted on Facebook under #StudiesofLight. As more friends and associates commented favorably on them, I felt encouraged to transfer the photos I had taken into a coffee table book. Through the help of many friends and their excellent ideas, it has evolved into an interesting way to see how light performs in a variety of environments and how it can be transferred to the stage.

Many friends suggested this is worth sharing by way of a literary effort. Writing this has been a labor of love. Through this process, I have revisited fond memories of the productions as well as use the design skills with which I have been gratefully gifted in authoring this book. I wrote it at a time when the world was in the grip of Covid-19. The project kept my design skills sharp and, more important, gave me something to do. May it be as enjoyable for you to read as it was for me to write.

Light is all around us. It permeates our lives. It affects our perceptions, outlooks, dispositions, and moods. Consider your mood on a sunny day versus a rainy one. Imagine a bright, delightful day at the beach juxtaposed against an intimate evening in front of a cozy fire. How does each one make you feel?

Part of my job as a freelance theatrical-lighting designer is to observe how light works in a multitude of scenarios. While doing so, I am researching how to represent it accurately on stage, thus making light an invaluable aid to my designs, to advance meaning and evoke emotions.

The purpose of this book is to demonstrate through images how light works in its many manifestations. Most of us take light for granted. Greater awareness of what light contributes to humankind's needs is a helpful conduit toward the betterment of our existence.

Enjoy this magical journey through the medium of light!

Introduction to Lighting Types

Light inspires me. I study it. I research it. I want to understand how it appears in natural and in artificial environments, so I can create the same effect on a stage. Light emphasizes emotion and evokes mood. It can clarify the actors' performance and further the playwright's meaning for the benefit and pleasure of the audience.

In the section that follows, you will see photographs of light in a variety of places, and then you can compare how I transferred that visual impact to a place and situation for an audience.

Natural Sources

A blazing sun, a blue-kissed moon, a calming candle, a crackling fire — all are natural sources of light. Portraying, or implying, natural sources of light in the theater can often lend itself to exciting abstractions.

Sunset

Miss Saigon, Manatee Performing Arts Center, Bradenton, FL, August 2014

Sunlight

Tarzan, Manatee Performing Arts Center, Bradenton, FL, August 2014

Sunlight and shadow

As with the previous two pages, these images demonstrate the power of silhouette and, in the theater image, shadow.

Sunset

Into the Woods, Orlando Shakespeare Theater, Orlando, FL, September 2006
(Photo courtesy of Rob Jones)

Moonlight

Tarzan, Manatee Performing Arts Center, Bradenton, FL, August 2014

Moonlight

A Little Night Music, Manatee Performing Arts Center, Bradenton, FL, October 2017

Candlelight

Suor Angelica, Opera Tampa, Straz Center,
Ferguson Hall, Tampa, FL, February 2009
(Photo courtesy of Opera Tampa/Straz Center)

Candlelight

A Little Night Music, Manatee Performing Arts Center, Bradenton, FL, October 2017

39 Steps, American Stage Theater Company, St. Petersburg, FL, November 2015 (Photo courtesy of American Stage Theatre Company)

An example of the abstraction of natural light—in this instance, firelight.
Note the red lighting to simulate the illumination generated by flames.

Firelight

Campfire (iStock by Getty Images)

Hunchback of Notre Dame, Manatee Performing Arts Center, Bradenton, FL, February 2018

Notice how the light on each discrete drop of water creates a self-contained universe.

Follies, Players Centre for the Performing Arts, Sarasota, FL, March 2019 (Photo courtesy of Don Daly Photo)

Into the Woods, Orlando Shakespeare Theater, Orlando, FL, September 2006 (Photo courtesy of Rob Jones)

In these examples, lighting creates discrete universes within the scene setting.

Beauty and the Beast,
Manatee Performing Arts
Center, Bradenton, FL,
December 2016

Les Miserables, Manatee
Performing Arts Center,
Bradenton, FL, August 2013

Opposite page below: The blue and red lighting in the foreground implies that the illumination is streaming in through the stained-glass windows.

Stained glass window, Gloria Dei Lutheran Church, St. Petersburg, FL.

Hosch
Theatre Lobby,
Gainesville
Theatre
Alliance,
University
of Northern
Georgia
and Brenau
University,
Gainesville, GA

Opposite page: *Faust*, Opera Tampa, Straz Center, Carol Morsani Hall, Tampa, FL, April 2009
(Photo courtesy of Opera Tampa/Straz Center)

Right: Cat dapple;
below: *Mousetrap*,
STAGEWORKS Theater,
ampa, FL, March 2019
(Photo courtesy of Scott Cooper)

Dock dapple

Into the Woods, Straz Center, Patel Conservatory, TECO Theatre, Tampa, FL, April 2016

Rainbow

Nine Parts of Desire,
Straz Center, Shimberg
Theatre, Tampa, FL,
March 2007

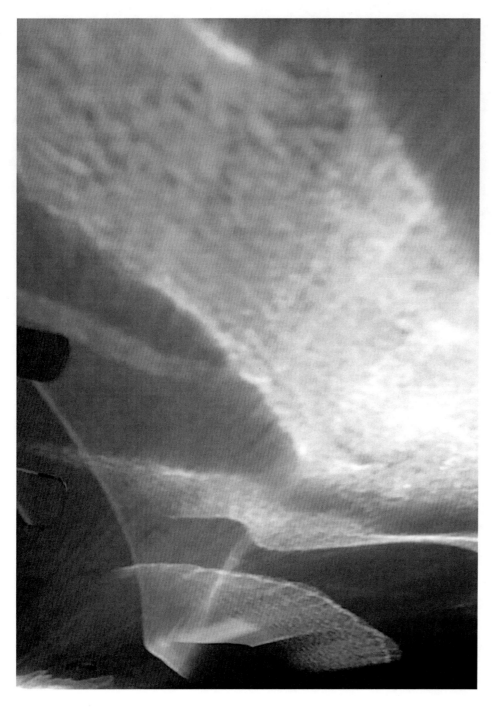

Light reflected on ceiling

Artificial Sources

*A*rtificial light sources are those manufactured to serve general or specific purposes.

LED PAR unit

Various types of incandescent, halogen, and fluorescent bulbs

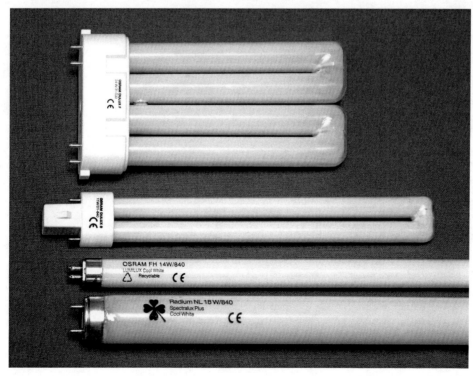

Fluorescent tubes (Photo courtesy Christian Taube, Wikipedia)

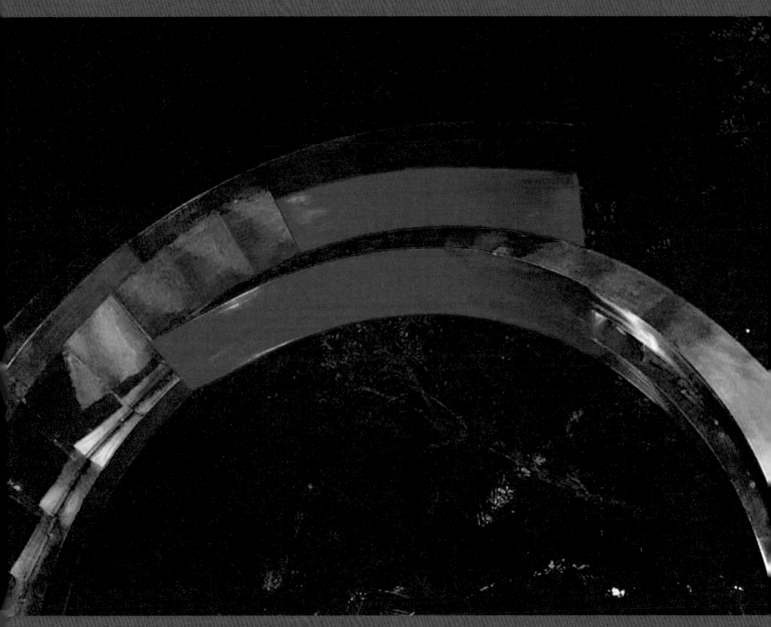

O Wave, sculpture by Gordon Heuther, installed in 2009, Beach Drive, St. Petersburg, FL

Jesus Christ Superstar, University of Northern Colorado, Langworthy Theatre, Greeley, CO, February 2018 (Photo courtesy of David Grapes)

Light-accented plant, Bonefish Grill, Bradenton, FL, August 2019

Little Shop of Horrors, Manatee Performing Arts Center, Bradenton, FL, January 2017

La Cage aux Folles, Riverfront Theater, Bradenton, FL, May 2009

St. Tropez, French Riviera (iStock by Getty Images)

Light sculpture, Coastal Eye Institute, Dr. Pooja Khator, Bradenton, FL

Godspell, Gainesville Theatre Alliance, Gainesville, GA, February 2017 (Photo courtesy of D. Connor McVey)

Warp-speed Christmas
decorations, Joseph Oshry
residence, November 2018

The Royale, American Stage Theater Company, St. Petersburg, FL, September 2017

Garden lighting, Motorworks Brewing Company, Bradenton, FL, November 2019

Cats, Manatee Performing Arts Center, Bradenton, FL, August 2015

My One and Only, Manatee Performing Arts Center, Bradenton, FL, May 2014

The special LED device used to create the lighting effect shown at left. It is known as an IColor Cove EC, manufactured by Color Kinetics.

Jesus Christ Superstar, University of Northern Colorado, Langworthy Theatre, Greeley, CO, February 2018. (Photo courtesy of David Grapes)

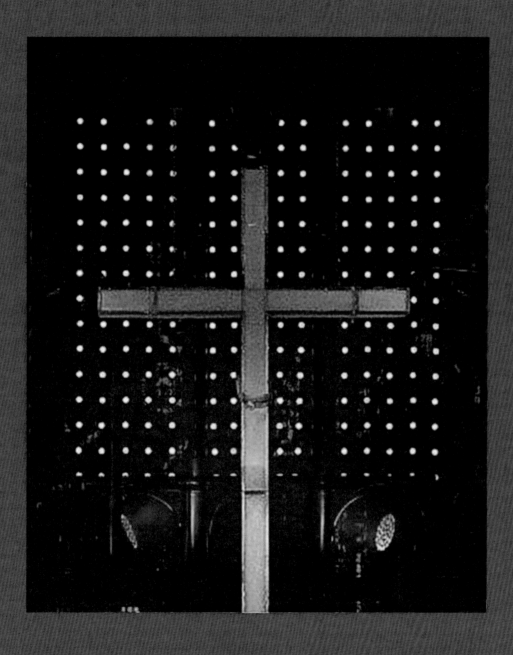

Shout!,
Manatee
Performing
Arts Center,
Bradenton, FL,
March 2011

Light Patterns

ight patterns are an arrangement of natural and/or artificial illumination and shadow on a surface.

These are created on stage using what is called a *gobo*, or "go between," of thin metal or glass secured into a slot — the *gobo holder* — with the desired pattern cut out to make the image. The technician secures the gobo at the focal point of specific lighting fixtures, between the light source and the lens. Gobos come in a variety of sizes and an assortment of images. In the film and photography industries, a gobo is called a "cookaloris" or "cookie."

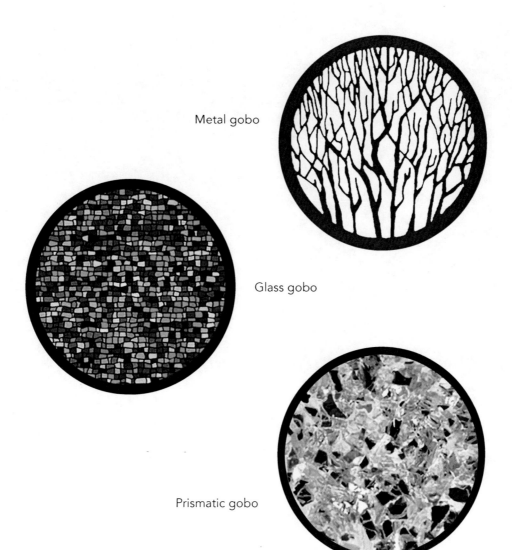

Metal gobo

Glass gobo

Prismatic gobo

Window pattern

Around the World in 80 Days, American Stage Theater
Company, St. Petersburg, FL, March 2014

Bridge
pattern

Sea grapes

The Roommate, American Stage Theater Company, St. Petersburg, FL, March 2019 (Photo courtesy of Steven K. Mitchell)

Leaf pattern

Singin' in the Rain, Athens Theatre, DeLand, FL, April 2019 (Photo courtesy of Mike Kitaif)

Bomb-itty of Errors, American Stage in the Park,
St. Petersburg, FL, April 2005

Stair pattern

Sarasota International Dance Festival, Sarasota Opera House, Sarasota, FL, August 2013

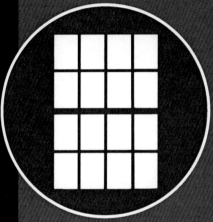

Window pattern, University Town Center Mall, Sarasota, FL, July 2019

Sarasota International Dance Festival, Sarasota Opera House, Sarasota, FL, August 2013

Slanted shutter pattern

John and
Mable
Ringling
Museum of
Art Courtyard,
2018,
Sarasota,
FL (Photo
courtesy
of Marian
Wallace)

Man of La Mancha, Players Centre of the Performing Arts, Sarasota, FL, February 2006

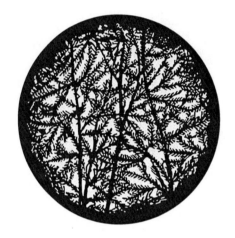

Morning striations

Cat GOBO

Godspell, Straz Center, Jaeb Theater, Tampa, FL, February 2010 (Photo courtesy of Mike Wood)

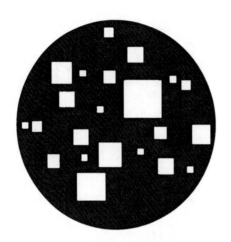

Breakup pattern, Indianapolis International Airport, Indianapolis, IN

Around the World in 80 Days, Florida Repertory Theatre, Ft. Myers, FL, February 2015

Translucents

*T*ranslucents transmit and/or diffuse light through a surface so objects behind the material cannot be seen clearly.

Fences,
American
Stage Theater
Company,
St. Petersburg,
FL, September
2009

Moon for the Misbegotten, American Stage Theater Company, St. Petersburg, FL, October 2003

Rain-soaked
window

Cobweb (Photo courtesy of Cory Boyas)

Kiss of the Spider Woman, Riverfront Theatre, Bradenton, FL, January 2000

Translucent drapery

Roméo et Juliette, Opera Tampa, Straz Center, Morsani Hall, Tampa, FL, December 2006
(Photo courtesy of Opera Tampa/Straz Center)

The King and I,
Riverfront
Theatre,
Bradenton, FL,
January 2004

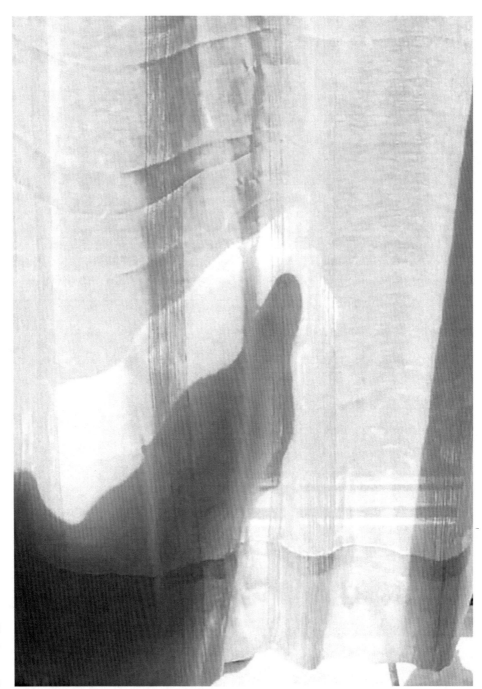

Shadow cat
(Photo
courtesy of C.
David Frankel)

Jekyll and Hyde, Athens Theatre, DeLand, FL, September 2018. (Photo courtesy of Mike KItaif)

Silhouettes

A *silhouette* is a shadow with a defined shape and dark outline created by placing the person or object in front of a light surface.

Sunset silhouette (Photo courtesy of Michael A. Oshry)

Coppelia, Interlochen Arts Academy, Interlochen, MI, December 2000

Willy Wonka Jr., Straz Center, Patel Conservatory in Ferguson Hall, Tampa, FL, August 2009

Cat in window

The Fantasticks, Hat Trick Theatre Company, Hudson, FL, April 2010

Circus performers (Photo courtesy of Jamie Lee Butrum)

Lamp in window

Jesus Christ Superstar, University of Northern Colorado, Langworthy Theatre, Greeley, CO, February 2018 (Photo courtesy of David Grapes)

Building silhouettes, St. Petersburg, FL

An American Dream, Straz Center, Ferguson Hall, Tampa, FL, May 2009

Light in the Sky

Light in the sky is a dominant element of our daily life. It often influences our mood and actions. A bright, sunny day affects us differently than a dark, overcast one. On the stage, light in the sky is often an important scenic element for establishing mood and tone.

God's work (Photo courtesy of Dee Oshry)

Turandot, Opera Tampa, Straz Center, Carol Morsani Hall, Tampa, FL, April 2004
(Photo courtesy of Opera Tampa/Straz Center)

Power clouds

Tosca, Palm Beach Opera, Kravis Center, West Palm Beach, FL, March 2011

A Doll's House, American
Stage Theater Company,
St. Petersburg, FL,
November 2012

Angry Zeus

Dear World, Players Centre for the Performing Arts, Sarasota, FL, January 2012

Aida, Riverfront Theater, Bradenton, FL, February 2012

Water

Images of how light looks on water.

Reflections on water

Aida, Lakeland Community Theatre,
Lakeland, FL, July 2013

Falling rain

Rain on water

Singin' in the Rain, Athens Theatre, DeLand, FL, April 2019 (Photo courtesy of Mike Kitaif)

Tarzan, Manatee Performing Arts Center, Bradenton, FL, August 2014

Ruby Falls

Fog and Haze

*F*og tends to be low lying, close to the floor. *Haze* fills an entire environment with water-based particulate, supplying a third dimension to a given visual.

Hazer

Fog machine

Equipment, Production Resource Group
(photos courtesy Mark Rabinowitz)

Cabaret, Theatre Winter Haven,
Winter Haven, FL, July, 1999

Roméo et Juliette, Opera Tampa, Straz Center, Morsani Hall, Tampa, FL, December 2006
(Photo courtesy of Opera Tampa/Straz Center)

Lake Superior morning

Into the Woods,
Orlando Shakespeare
Theater, Orlando, FL,
September 2006 (Photo
courtesy of Rob Jones)

Jekyll and Hyde, Athens Theatre, DeLand, FL,
September 2018 (Photo courtesy of Mike Kitaif)

Foggy trees
(Photo courtesy of Patty Cleary)

Point Reyes National Seashore, Marin County, CA (Photo courtesy of Kim Northrop)

The Secret Garden, Manatee Performing Arts Center, Bradenton, FL, September 2015

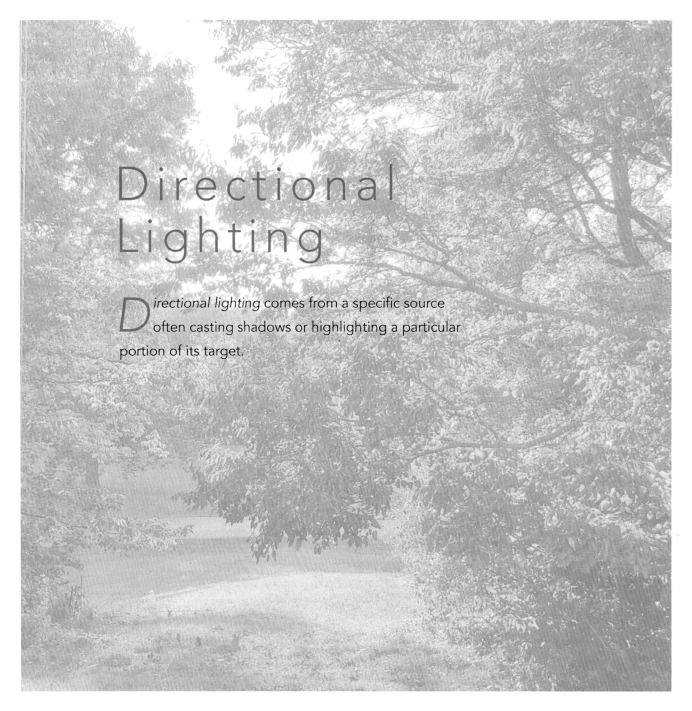

Directional Lighting

*D*irectional lighting comes from a specific source often casting shadows or highlighting a particular portion of its target.

Jekyll and Hyde, Athens Theatre, DeLand, FL, September 2018 (Photo courtesy of Mike Kitaif)

Skeleton Crew, American Stage Theatre Company, St. Petersburg, FL, January 2020 (Photo courtesy of American Stage Theatre Company

Casa Blue, American Stage Theatre Company, St. Petersburg, FL, July 2007

Tree pool (Photo courtesy of Martin R. Petlock)

The Royale, American Stage Theatre Company, St. Petersburg, FL, September 2017

Lit trees

Willy Wonka Jr., Straz Center, Patel Conservatory, Tampa, FL, August 2009

Naming True, Urbanite Theatre, Sarasota, FL,
May 2017 (Photo courtesy of Dylan Jon Wade Cox)

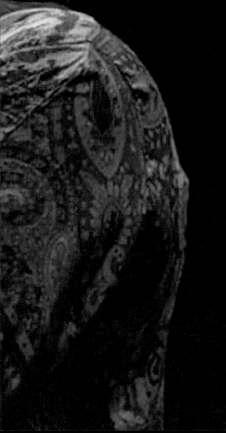

Side light (Photo courtesy of Heath Lane)

135

Uplighting

Assassins, Manatee Performing Arts Center, Bradenton, FL, October 2016

Page to Stage

This section walks you through the process of stage lighting design as well as giving you a peek behind the scenes.

Chess, Manatee Performing Arts Center, Stone Hall, Bradenton, FL, February 2016

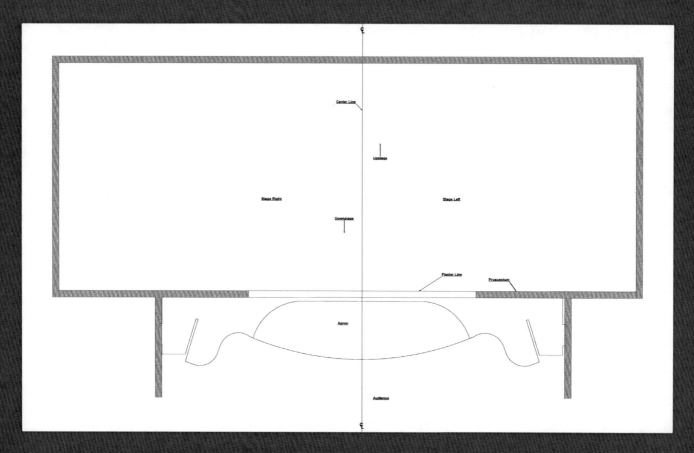

Center Lines and Plaster Lines

A *centerline* is drawn on a scenic designer's floor plan and a lighting designer's light plot. It bisects the stage from the center of the proscenium arch and extends downstage to the apron and upstage to the theater's back wall.

A *plaster line* is typically reserved for proscenium theaters. It is a line drawn from the upstage side of the proscenium arch laterally to the opposite side of the arch.

Proscenium Arch

Follies, Players Centre for the Performing Arts, Sarasota, FL, March 2019 (Photo courtesy of Ken Junkins)

Lighting design development in progress (AKA where the magic begins)

On set (AKA where the magic happens)

19

EARLY MORNING

Scene Two

(In darkness, the humming of machinery creates a midwest hip-hop score. It is an extension of the factory line soundtrack that opened the play.)

(Silhouetted workers are seen in action – their factory line dance.)

(Suddenly, a chink in the machinery. The workers repeat movements as if they are stuck between two motions – unable to complete their task. Short circuiting – caught in dysfunction.)

(Lights crossfade onto the breakroom.)

(It is early morning. Sunlight spills into the windows. Clothes are lying around on the floor and the dilapidated couch. A locker is partially open. The heater is on.)

(DEZ enters the breakroom wearing a coat and backpack. Walks over to a boombox resting on a crate. Unplugs the heater and plugs in the boombox. Puts on a CD. Slum Village, "Get Dis Money.")

(Notices the clothes that are lain about. The open locker. Registers it questionably.)

(Takes out his hard boots. Chan... his nice gym shoes. Puts gym shoes i... off backpack. Looks around hims... from his hip. Places it in his ba... it good.)

14 — SCENE LIGHT SL
15 — ADD SRC

A license to produce SKELETON CREW does... license for "Get Dis Money" by Slum Village... suggest that the licensee contact ASCAP or... publisher and contact such music publi... permission for performance of the song... unattainable for "Get Dis Money," the lic... SKELETON CREW but may create an ori... style. For further information, please see...

144

PRESK...
NARRATOR: LET TH...
BEGINNING OF...

1. **PROLOGUE**

SOME FOLKS DREAM OF...
BEFORE THEIR TIME...
SOME JUST DON'T HA...
THEY HIDE THEIR HO...
NOW I DON'T SAY WH...
BUT IF BY CHANCE...
THEN ALL I NEED...
TO TELL THE TALE...

WE ALL DREAM A LO...
SOME ARE LUCKY,...
BUT IF YOU THINK...
THEN IT'S REAL...
YOU ARE WHAT YOU...

BUT ALL THAT I S...
IN THE STORY OF...
AND HE COULD BE...

2. **ANY DREAM W...**

I CLOSED MY EY...
DREW BACK THE...
TO SEE FOR CE...
WHAT I THOUGH...
FAR FAR AWAY...
SOMEONE WAS...
BUT THE WORL...
ANY DREAM WI...

I WORE MY COAT
WITH GOLDEN LINING
BRIGHT COLOURS SHINING
WONDERFUL AND NEW
AND IN THE EAST
THE DAWN WAS BREAKING
THE WORLD WAS WAKING

ADD CHORUS

Joseph and the Amazing Technicolor Dreamcoat libretto...

---

1 — 1+W
2 — TIME C...
SUB 6 CURT SPACE
SUB 6 OUT
3 — 47½
4 — 147 6
5 — STL OUT
6 — WINDOWS GT

Light Plot

A *light plot* is a schematic showing stage electricians where to hang each light for the show. Creating it is part of the design development process. As well as each light's position, the light plot specifies what it does, what color it is, the control channel assigned to it, and what, if any, gobos are required.

I use VectorWorks, a drafting program made by the Nemetschek Group, whose software products include a specific module for stage-lighting design. My drawings are typically in ½" scale, and I indicate the critical elements of centerline and plaster line.

For more specific detail, I use Lightwright, a proprietary software developed by John McKernon, to work in conjunction with the light plot. This application manages theatrical lighting data and paperwork and prints out a variety of schedules. Both VectorWorks and Lightwright can transfer data from one application to the other. If I make a change in one application, the other reflects it. This allows me to make accurate paperwork and check my progress as I go through a process.

Magic Sheet

A *magic sheet* is a drawing I develop using VectorWorks, to be my quick reference guide after design development moves into the theater. The sheet shows where each light is located and what it does. I can see at a glance which lights or series of lights are doing what, plus their color and gobo indication. This document allows me to work rapidly and make the most effective use of the time allowed inside the theater to build the show's light cues.

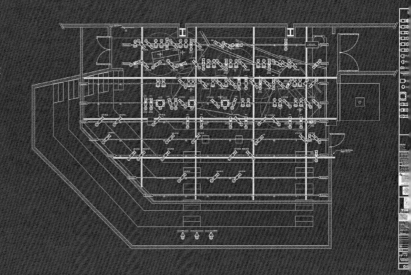

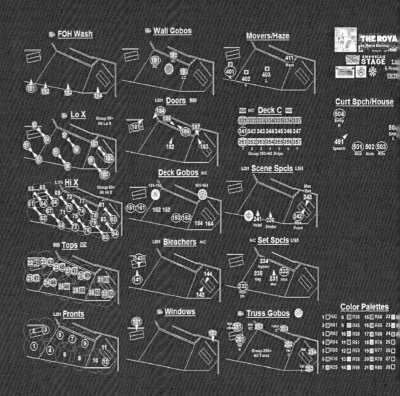

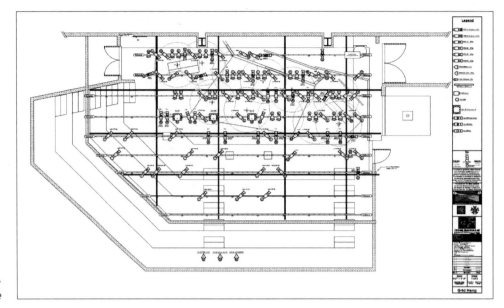

Light plot,
The Royale

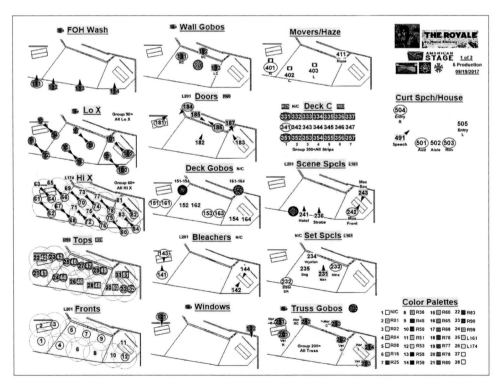

Magic sheet,
The Royale

The Royale,
American Stage
Theatre Company,
St. Petersburg, FL,
September 2017

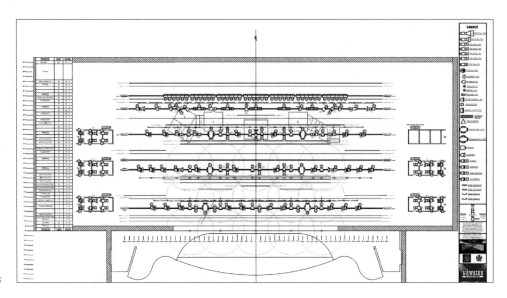

Light plot,
Newsies

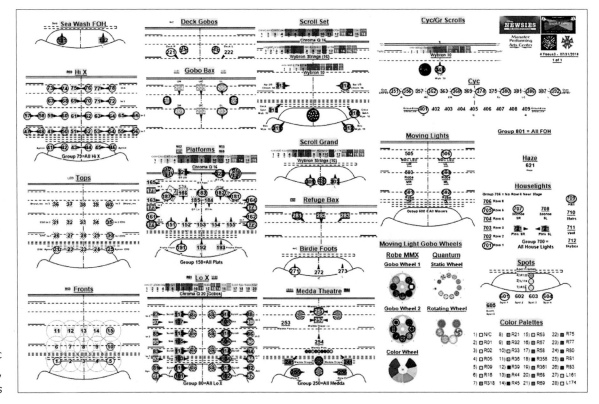

Magic
sheet,
Newsies

Newsies, Manatee Performing Arts Center, Bradenton, FL. July 2018

Newsies, Manatee Performing Arts Center, Bradenton, FL, July 2018

Sample script index for *Newsies*

American Buffalo, Palm Beach Dramaworks, set under work light, West Palm Beach, FL, November 2010

American Buffalo, Palm Beach Dramaworks, set under stage light, West Palm Beach, FL, November 2010

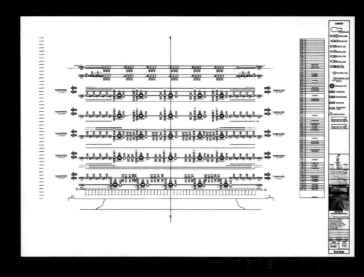

Light plot

Lady Swanwhite, Straz Center, Ferguson Hall, Tampa, FL, February 2019
(Photo by Will Staples, Courtesy of Opera Tampa/Straz Center for the Performing Arts)

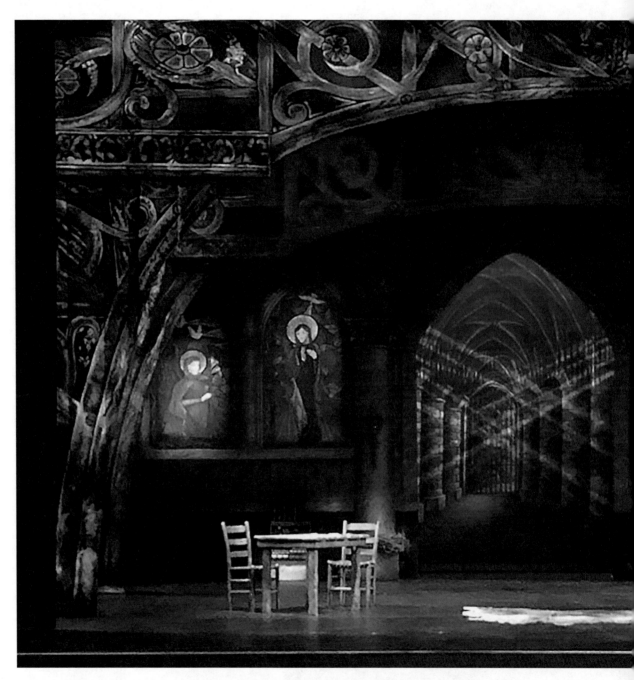

Lady Swanwhite, Straz Center, Ferguson Hall, Tamps, FL, February 2019 (Photo courtesy of Kristin Coppola)

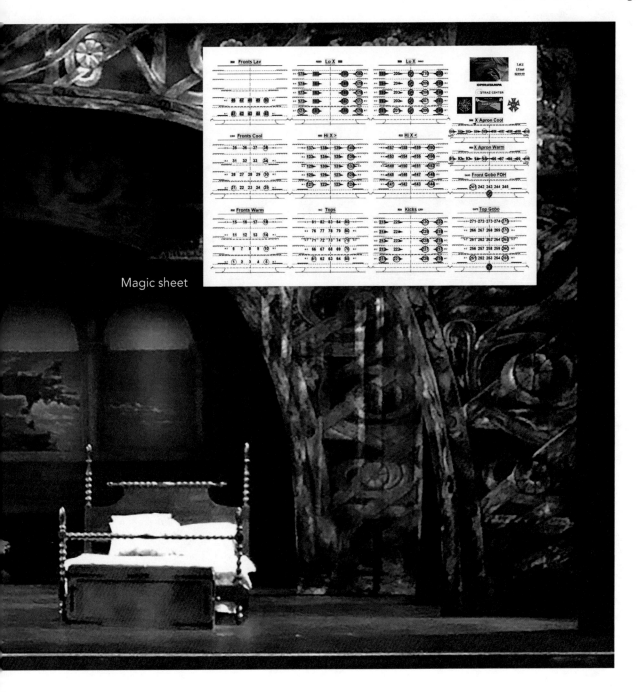

Magic sheet

Front of house, Players Centre for the Performing Arts, Sarasota, FL. This shows the front of house lighting position at the Players Centre for the Performing Arts as seen from the stage

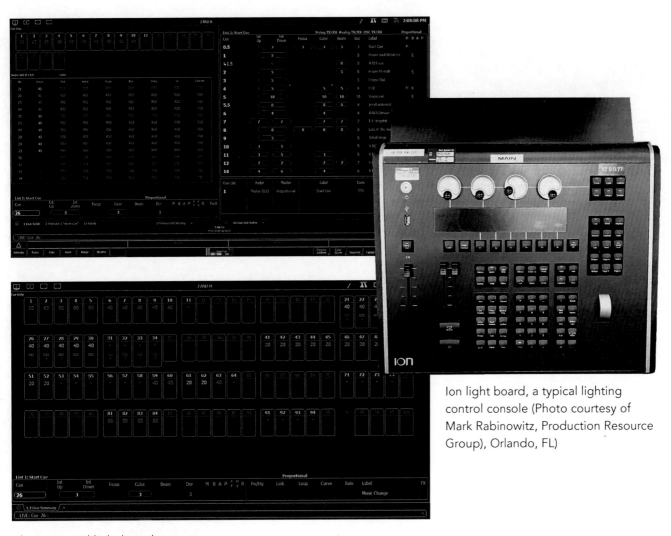

Ion light board, a typical lighting control console (Photo courtesy of Mark Rabinowitz, Production Resource Group), Orlando, FL)

Above: typical light board screens

Light Cue Sheet, *Doors*

A Light Cue Sheet tracks the light cues for shows. Listed are the cue number, fade time, cue attributes, script page number, and a brief description of each cue's purpose.

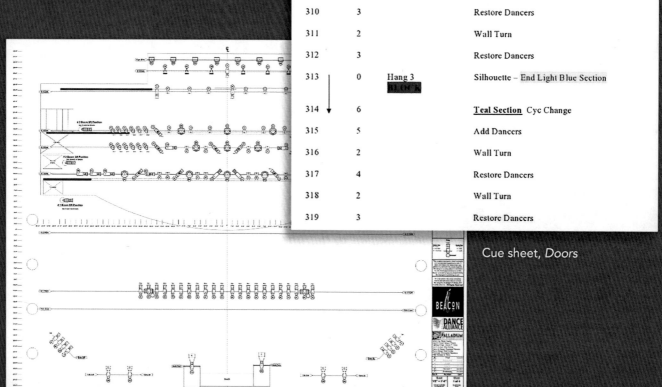

Doors

08/23/19   Page 1 of 3

Beacon 2019 - Palladium Theatre
Light Cues

Cue	Time	Attribute	Page	Description
301	5			Preset
302	5			House to Half
303	5	Fol 4		House Out
304	5	BLOCK		Cyc Out
305	7			**Light Blue Section** – Add Cyc – Dancers Enter
306	5			Dancers Expand R/L
307	1			Wall Turn
308	2			Restore Dancers
309	1			Wall Turn
310	3			Restore Dancers
311	2			Wall Turn
312	3			Restore Dancers
313	0	Hang 3 BLOCK		Silhouette – End Light Blue Section
314	6			**Teal Section** Cyc Change
315	5			Add Dancers
316	2			Wall Turn
317	4			Restore Dancers
318	2			Wall Turn
319	3			Restore Dancers

Cue sheet, *Doors*

Light plot, *Doors*

Doors, Palladium Theatre, St. Petersburg, FL, April 2019. (Photo courtesy of Tom Kramer)

Caravan Stage Company produced *Nomadic Tempest* in April 2017, a seventy-five minute, one-act show. It is about four Monarch butterflies struggling to survive in 2040, after fossil-fuel consumption destroys our climate.

The stage was the deck of the *Amara Zee*, a tall ship. Paul Kirby is the vessel's captain and also served as the show's artistic director. Production work was carried out in Tampa Bay, and performances were presented outdoors at four ports on James Island in Canada, in the sovereign territory of the Saanich people.

Nomadic Tempest, Tall Ship *Amara Zee,* St. Petersburg, FL, April 2017

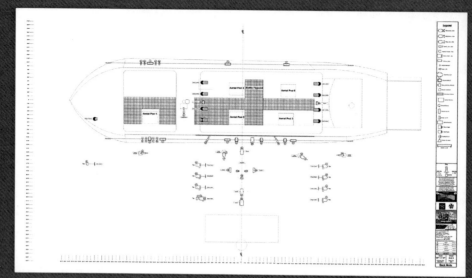

Light plot,
*Nomadic
Tempest*

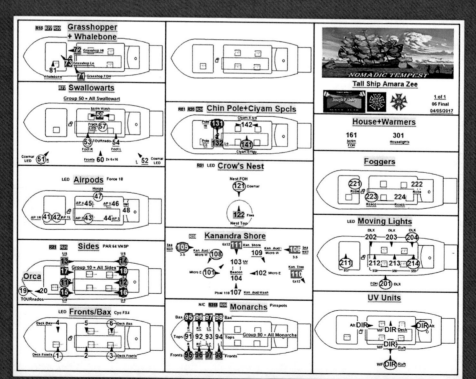

Magic sheet,
*Nomadic
Tempest*

164

Tall Ship *Amara Zee*, St. Petersburg, FL, April 2017

Nomadic Tempest, Tall Ship *Amara Zee*,
St. Petersburg, FL, April 2017

Lighting Terms

Incandescent: Adjective.
in·can·des·cent | \ in-kn-de- snt
An *incandescent* light source is one where
a wire filament is heated to such a high
temperature, it glows with visible light
(*incandescence*). A glass bulb filled with an
inert gas is sealed around the filament.

Fluorescent: Adjective.
fluo·res·cent | \ flu-re-snt
Fluorescence is the emission of light
by a substance that has absorbed light
or other electromagnetic radiation. It is a
form of luminescence. In most cases, the
emitted light has a longer wavelength,
and therefore lower energy, than the
absorbed radiation.

LED: (Adjective. lehd. Acronym
for Light-Emitting Diode.
A LED lamp or *LED light bulb* is an
electric light that produces illumination by
using one or more light-emitting diodes.
LED lamps have a lifespan many times
longer than incandescent lamps and are
significantly more efficient than most other
artificial light sources.

Degrees Kelvin: Noun. kel·vin | \ kel-vn
The measurement for *color temperature,*
the appearnce of warmth or coolness
provided by a light bulb.

Diffusion: Noun. dif·fu·sion | \ di-fyü-zhn
The even spreading of illumination from
a light source evenly to reduce glare and
harsh shadows. Designed to soften sharp
outlines in light.

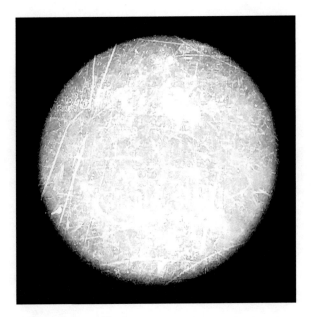

Light without diffusion

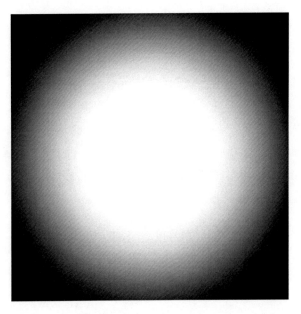

Light with diffusion

Color temperature

About the Author

A resident of Florida since 1986, Joseph P. Oshry has designed lighting for over 590 productions with such cultural heavyweights as the Asolo Repertory Theatre, American Stage Theatre Company, Wick Theatre, Palm Beach DramaWorks, Maltz Jupiter Theatre, Gainesville Theatre Alliance, Atlanta Lyric Theatre, Orlando-UCF Shakespeare Theatre, Florida Repertory Theatre, Urbanite Theatre, Palm Beach Opera, Opera Tampa, New Orleans Opera, Sarasota Opera, Carreno Dance Festival, Sarasota International Dance Festival, Ballet Eddy Toussaint USA (now Ballet Eddy Toussaint), and the Interlochen Dance Ensemble in Michigan.

Joseph Oshry has also provided lighting for such personalities as Madeleine Sherwood, Rita Gardner, Wynton Marsalis, Michael Franks, and the late Burl Ives.

Joseph has twenty world-premiere productions to his credit, covering theatre, musicals, dance pieces, and two new operas, *Sacco and Vanzetti* and *Lady Swanwhite*, both written by Anton Coppola.

Joseph's consultation projects include designing the lighting system for the new theatre of the American Stage Theatre Company in St. Petersburg as well as the recently constructed Manatee Performing Arts Center in Bradenton.

He has been an advisor for equipment purchases for theatres and other organizations throughout Florida. His clients have implemented Joseph's recommendations regarding the newer ETC Eos family of lighting consoles as well as for the latest in LED and moving light equipment.

Joseph is the recipient of Individual Artist Fellowships in 1997 and 2007. He served as a theatre panelist for the 1999–2000 grant period. In addition, he has won four Theatre Tampa Bay awards for outstanding lighting design for *The Mystery of Irma Vep*, *The Royale*, and *The Rocky Horror Picture Show* at the American Stage Theatre Company in St. Petersburg, FL, as well as for *In the Time of the Butterflies* at StageWorks Theatre in Tampa, FL. Recently he received a Design Excellence award for his work on *Jesus Christ Superstar* at the University of Northern Colorado, presented by the Kennedy Center, American College Theatre Festival. He has been a member of IATSE Local 412, Sarasota, since 1987, and of United Scenic Artists Local 829, New York, since 1991. He serves on the Artistic Advisory Board for Tampa Repertory Theatre.

Joseph lives in Bradenton with his wife, Denise, and is proud to have been married to her for over thirty years.

Labor Organizations

United Scenic Artists Local USA-829

United Scenic Artists, Local USA 829, IATSE, is a labor union and professional association of Designers, Artists, Craftspeople, and Department Coordinators, organized to protect craft standards, working conditions and wages for the entertainment and decorative arts industries. The members of Local USA 829 work in film, theatre, opera, ballet, television, industrial shows, commercials and exhibitions. The current active membership totals over 4,800.

United Scenic Artists, Local USA 829, is a national organization maintaining business offices in New York, Chicago and Los Angeles. The business of the Local is conducted by National Business Agent, and her staff, out of the main office in New York City and two Regional Business Representatives in Chicago (Central Region) and Los Angeles (Western Region). In addition to the New York staff, the Eastern Region also has Business Representatives in Boston and Washington, DC. For more information visit the International Alliance of Theatrical Stage Employees website via https://www.usa829.org/.

IATSE Local 412

The International Alliance of Theatrical Stage Employees, Moving Picture Technicians, Artists and Allied Crafts of the United States, its Territories and Canada, AFL-CIO, CFC.

A Mixed Stagehands Local Union whose jurisdiction covers Bradenton, Sarasota, and Venice, Florida. Founded in 1925, Local 412 provides professional, highly skilled labor consisting of those who do the work of the theatre. Members are also skilled in television, film, scenic studios, and outdoor venues. Some areas of expertise include audio technicians, carpenters, and electricians as well as wardrobe, rigging, and special-effects personnel. For more information visit the International Alliance of Theatrical Stage Employees website via https://www.iatse.net/.

Actors' Equity Association

Established in 1913, Actors' Equity Association is the United States-based labor organization representing actors and stage managers who number among over 51,000 members. Actors' Equity is a member of and working under the auspices of the AFL-CIO and is also affiliated with the Ferderation Internationale Artistes (FIA).

Actors' Equity's mission is based in unity of purpose and respective support of its membership working toward common goal and consistent policy. All members, governed by its National Council, strive to make safe and comfortable working environments, in addition to providing pension and health insurance for its members. For more information, visit the Equity website at www.actorsequity.org

Acknowledgments

Many thanks to all the Producers, Artistic Directors, Production Directors, Fellow Designers, Production Support Personnel, and Performers who brought this book to life. Thanks to Concept Editor Kim Northrop for helping me tie photographs from the world to production photos, supplying the subtitle "In the World and on the Stage," and recommending the Page to Stage section. Her website is www.kimnorthrop.com. Thanks to Laurie Rosin for her brilliant text editing and for teaching me the difference between Active and Passive writing. Her website is www.thebookeditor.com. Thanks to Ron Toelke for his excellent graphic and publication design skills, along with his recommendations toward making the book more visually appealing. His website is www.toelkeassociates.com.

Thanks to J. William Ruyle for the Foreword, along with his daughters Nancy Paul and Wendy Ruyle for their skillful proofreading of the Foreword. Thanks to the photographers who gave me permission to use their work in this book, in particular Mike Kitaif (www.mikekit.com), Dylan Jon Wade Cox (www.djwcphoto.com), Will Staples (www.willstaplesphotography.com), and Tom Kramer (www.tkramerphoto.com).

Thanks to all for their suggestions: S. K. Randolph, Tom Krantz, Michael A. Oshry, J. William Ruyle, Christopher Baldwin, M. Alan Oshry, Martin R. Petlock, Ranney M. Lawrence, Rick Kerby, Jeffery Kin, Jamie Lee Butrum, Cory Boyas, Todd Olson, Christopher McVicker, Rob Jones, Anne Hering, Kristin Coppola, Robert de Warren, Stephanie Gularte, Roman Black, and Martina Smith.

Thanks to Tyrell Foster at Rosco International (us.rosco.com/en) for his permission to use Gobo images and to Mark Rabinowitz at Production Resource Group (PRG) for his help in generating images for fog and haze machines (www.prg.com/en). Thanks to Doug Cherry, Attorney with Shumaker Law, Sarasota, FL, for making sure all content is presented legally. Most certainly thanks to my parents, Curt and Barbara Daniels, along with friends and family for supporting this endeavor, particularly my wife, Dee Oshry.

Credits

Front Cover: *Miss Saigon,* Manatee Performing Arts Center, Bradenton, FL, March 2013. Artistic Director/Director: Rick Kerby, Scenic Design: Marc Lalosh, Costume Design: David Walker and Georgina Willmott.

Title Page: *A Little Night Music,* Manatee Performing Arts Center, Bradenton, FL, October 2017. Artistic Director/Director: Rick Kerby, Scenic Design: Kenneth Mooney, Costume Design: Becky Evans. Actors depicted: (left) Bridget Marsh (Fredrika Armfeldt), (right) Jeanne Larranaga (Madame Armfeldt). Photo courtesy of Manatee Performing Arts Center.

Table of Contents Page: *Gaspar Ballet,* Straz Center, Ferguson Hall, Tampa, FL, January 2012. Choreographer: Christopher Fleming. Scenic Design: Tandova Studios, Costume Design: Camille McClellan.

Page iv: *Fireworks,* Photo courtesy of Amy Oshry.

Page vi: *Alma Mater,* Photo courtesy of Illinois State University.

Page viii: *Madama Butterfly,* Opera Tampa, Straz Center, Carol Morsani Hall, Tampa, FL, November 2004. Director: James Marvel, Scenic Design supplied by Palm Beach Opera. Costumes supplied by Malabar. Photo courtesy of Opera Tampa/Straz Center.

Pages 4–5: *Miss Saigon,* Manatee Performing Arts Center, Bradenton, FL, August 2014. Artistic Director/Director: Rick Kerby, Scenic Design: Marc Lalosh, Costume Design: David Walker and Georgina Wilmott.

Pages 6–7: *Tarzan,* Manatee Performing Arts Center, Bradenton, FL, August 2014. Artistic Director/Director: Rick Kerby, Scenic Design: Dan Yerman, Costume Design: Becky Evans. Actors depicted: (front) Dave Downer, Jr. (Kerchak), (back) MaryKate D. Glidewell (Kala).

Pages 8–9: *Into the Woods,* Orlando Shakespeare Theater in partnership with University of Central Florida, Orlando, FL, September 2006. Artistic Director: Jim Helsinger, Director: Patrick Flick, Scenic Design: Bert Scott+, Costume Design: Rebecca Turk, Actor depicted: Robbie Sharpe*(Jack). Photo courtesy of Rob Jones.

Page 11: *Tarzan,* Manatee Performing Arts Center, Bradenton, FL, August 2014. Artistic Director/Director: Rick Kerby, Scenic Design: Dan Yerman, Costume Design: Becky Evans. Actors depicted: (left) MaryKate D. Glidewell (Kala), (right) Dave Downer, Jr. (Kerchak).

Page 13: *A Little Night Music,* Manatee Performing Arts Center, Bradenton, FL, October 2017. Artistic Director/Director: Rick Kerby, Scenic Design: Kenneth Mooney, Costume Design: Becky Evans. Actors depicted: (left) Bridget Marsh (Fredrika Armfeldt), (right) Jeanne Larranaga (Madame Armfeldt). Photo courtesy of Manatee Performing Arts Center.

Page 15: *Suor Angelica,* Straz Center, Opera Tampa, Ferguson Hall, Tampa, FL, February 2009. Director: Joachim Schamberger, Scenic Design: Joachim Schamberger, Costumes: Malabar. Photo courtesy of Opera Tampa/Straz Center.

Page 17: *A Little Night Music,* Manatee Performing Arts Center, Bradenton, FL, October 2017. Artistic Director/Director: Rick Kerby, Scenic Design: Kenneth Mooney, Costume Design: Becky Evans.

Page 18: *The 39 Steps,* American Stage Theatre Company, St. Petersburg, FL, November 2015. Artistic Director/Director: Stephanie Gularte, Scenic Design: Jerid Fox, Costume Design: Catherine Cann, Actor depicted: Juliana Davis* (Annabella/Margaret/Pamela). Photo courtesy of American Stage Theatre Company.

Page 21: *Hunchback of Notre Dame,* Manatee Performing Arts Center, Bradenton, FL, February 2018. Artistic Director/Director: Rick Kerby, Scenic/Costume Design: Kenneth Mooney.

Page 24 Top: *Follies,* Players Centre for the Performing Arts, Sarasota, FL, March 2019. Artistic Director/Director: Jeffery Kin, Scenic Design: Ken Junkins, Costume Design: Georgina Wilmott. Actors depicted: (left) Jeanne Larranaga (Heidi Schiller), (center), Jaimi McPeek (Showgirl), (right) Eliza Engle-Morehouse (Young Heidi). Photo courtesy of Don Daly, www.dondalyphoto.com/.

Page 24 Bottom: *Into the Woods,* Orlando Shakespeare Theater in partnership with University of Central Florida, Orlando, FL, September 2006. Artistic Director: Jim Helsinger, Director: Patrick Flick, Scenic Design: Bert Scott+, Costume Design: Rebecca Turk. Actors depicted: (left) Heather Charles* (Baker's Wife), (right) Mary Candler (Rapunzel). Photo courtesy of Rob Jones.

Page 26 Top: *Beauty and the Beast,* Manatee Performing Arts Center, Bradenton, FL, December 2016. Artistic Director: Rick Kerby, Director: Cory Boyas, Scenic Design: Caleb Carrier, Costume Design: Becky Evans. Actors depicted: (right center) Dave Downer, Jr. (Beast), (left center) Melanie Bierweiler (Belle), (left front) Mark Eichorn (Cogsworth), (left back) Griffyn Holcomb (Lumiere).

Page 26 Bottom: *Les Miserables,* Manatee Performing Arts Center, Bradenton, FL, August 2013. Artistic Director/Director: Rick Kerby, Scenic Design: Kirk V. Hughes, Costume Design: David Walker.

Page 28: *Faust,* Opera Tampa, Straz Center, Carol Morsani Hall, Tampa, FL, April 2009. Director: David Lefkowich, Scenic Design: Alan Rusnack, Costumes: Malabar. Photo courtesy of Opera Tampa/Straz Center.

Page 30: *The Mousetrap,* StageWorks Theatre, Tampa, FL, March 2019. Artistic Director: Karla Hartley, Director: Paul Fino, Scenic Design: Scott Cooper+, Costume Design: Nadalia Morales. Photo courtesy of Scott Cooper.

Page 32: *Into the Woods,* Straz Center, Patel Conservatory, TECO Theatre, Tampa, FL, April 2016. Director: Suzanne Livesey, Scenic Design: Tom Hansen, Costume Design: Nicole Sharp.

Page 34: *Nine Parts of Desire,* Straz Center, Shimberg Theatre, Tampa, FL, March 2007. Co-Production with American Stage Theatre Company, St. Petersburg, FL. Artistic Director: Todd Olson, Director: Jorge Acosta, Scenic Design: Scott Cooper+, Costume Design: Adrin Puente. Actor depicted: Julie Rowe* (one actor playing multiple roles).

Page 39: *Jesus Christ Superstar,* University of Northern Colorado, Langworthy Theatre, February 2018. Director: David Grapes, Scenic Design: J David Blatt, Costume Design: Anne Toewe+. Photo courtesy of David Grapes.

Page 41: *Little Shop of Horrors,* Manatee Performing Arts Center, Bradenton, FL, January 2017. Artistic Director: Rick Kerby, Director: DeWayne Barrett, Scenic Design: Caleb Carrier, Costume Design: Becky Evans. Actor depicted: Craig Weiskerger (Seymour Krelborn).

Pages 42–43: *La Cage aux Folles,* Manatee Players, Riverfront Theatre, Bradenton, FL, May 2009. Director/Artistic Director: Rick Kerby, Scenic and Costume Design: Kenneth Mooney.

Page 43: St. Tropez, French Riviera. Photo iStock by Getty Images.

Page 45: *Godspell,* Gainesville Theatre Alliance, Gainesville, GA, February 2017. Scenic Design: Larry Cook. Photo courtesy of D. Connor McVey.

Page 47: *The Royale,* American Stage Theatre Company, St. Petersburg, FL, September 2017. Artistic Director: Stephanie Gularte, Director: Lisa Powers Tricomi, Scenic Design: Jerid Fox, Costume Design: Trish Kelley.

Page 49: *Cats,* Manatee Performing Arts Center, Bradenton, FL, August 2015. Artistic Director: Rick Kerby, Director: DeWayne Barrett, Scenic Design: Donna Buckalter, Costume Design: Becky Evans.

Pages 50–51: *My One and Only,* Manatee Performing Arts Center, Bradenton, FL, May 2014. Artistic Director/Director: Rick Kerby, Scenic and Costume Design: Kenneth Mooney.

Page 52–53: *Jesus Christ Superstar,* University of Northern Colorado, Langworthy Theatre, Greeley, CO, February 2018. Director: David Grapes, Scenic Design: J. David Blatt, Costume Design: Anne Toewe+. Photo courtesy of David Grapes.

Page 54–55: *Shout!,* Manatee Players, Riverfront Theatre, Bradenton, FL, March 2011. Artistic Director: Rick Kerby, Director: Cheryl Carty, Scenic Design: Donna Buckalter, Costume Design: Rick Kerby.

Pages 58–59: *Around the World in 80 Days,* American Stage Theatre Company, St. Petersburg, FL, March 2014. Artistic Director/Director: Todd Olson, Scenic Design: Jerid Fox, Costume Design: Kathy Buck.

Page 61: *The Roommate,* American Stage Theatre Company, St. Petersburg, FL, March 2019. Artistic Director: Stephanie Gularte, Director: Kristin Clippard, Scenic Design: Steven K. Mitchell+, Costume Design: Catherine Cann. Photo courtesy of Steven K. Mitchell.

Pages 62–63: *Singin' in the Rain,* Athens Theatre, DeLand, FL, April 2019. Artistic Director: Craig Uppercue, Directors: A. J. Garcia and C. J. Sikorski, Scenic Design: Craig Uppercue, Costume Design: Tamara Marke-Lares. Actors depicted: (left) Madeline Reiger (Kathy Seldon), (right) Nate Elliott (Don Lockwood). Photo courtesy of Mike Kitaif.

Page 64: *Bomb-itty of Errors,* American Stage in the Park, St. Petersburg, FL, April 2005. Director: Andrew Goldberg, Scenic Design: Mark Kobak, Costume Design: Amy Cianci. Actors depicted: (far left upper) Kevin Shand (D. J.), (lower left) "ranney"* (Antipholus of Ephesus), (right of center) Postell Pringle* (Dr. Pinch), (right) Christopher V. Edwards* (Luciana).

Pages 66–67: *Sarasota International Dance Festival,* Sarasota Opera House, August 2013. Producer: Robert de Warren, Artistic Director: Jose Manuel Carreno.

Page 68–69: *Sarasota International Dance Festival,* Sarasota Opera House, August 2013. Producer: Robert de Warren, Artistic Director: Jose Manuel Carreno.

Pages 70–71: *Man of La Mancha,* Players Centre for the Performing Arts, Sarasota, FL, February 2006. Director and Scenic Design: Jeff Dillon, Costume Design: Tim Beltey.

Page 73: *Godspell,* Straz Center, Jaeb Theater, Tampa, FL, February 2010. Director: Rick Criswell, Scenic Design: Scott Cooper+, Costume Design: Amy Cianci. Photo courtesy of Mike Wood.

Pages 74—75: *Around the World in 80 Days,* Florida Repertory Theatre, Ft. Myers, FL, February 2015. Artistic Director: Robert Cacioppo, Director: Mark Shanahan, Scenic Design: Richard Crowell.

Page 77: *Fences,* American Stage Theatre Company, St. Petersburg, FL, September 2009. Artistic Director: Todd Olson, Director: Timothy Douglass, Scenic Design: Jeffrey W. Dean+.

Page 78: *Moon for the Misbegotten,* American Stage Theatre Company, St. Petersburg, FL, October 2003. Artistic Director/Director: Todd Olson, Scenic Design: David M. Fillmore, Jr., Costume Design: Amy Cianci. Actor depicted: Julie Rowe* (Josie Hogan).

Page 81: *Kiss of the Spider Woman,* Manatee Players, Riverfront Theatre, Bradenton, FL, January 2000. Artistic Director: Rick Kerby, Director: Scott Keys, Scenic Design: Lars Paulson, Costume Design: Jean Brudevold. Actor depicted: Eve Marie Caballero (Spider Woman).

Page 82–83: *Roméo et Juliette,* Opera Tampa, Straz Center, Carol Morsani Hall, Tampa, FL, December 2006. Director: David Lefkowich, Scenic Design: Peter Dean Beck, Costumes: Utah Opera. Photo courtesy of Opera Tampa/Straz Center

Page 84–85: *The King and I,* Manatee Players, Riverfront Theatre, Bradenton, FL, January 2004. Artistic Director/Director: Rick Kerby, Scenic Design: Michael Gray, Costume Design: Nic Hartmann.

Page 87: *Jekyll and Hyde,* Athens Theatre, DeLand, FL. September 2018. Artistic Director: Craig Uppercue, Director: Trevor Southworth, Scenic Design: Tori Oakes, Costume Design: Tamara Marke-Lares. Actors depicted: (front) Trevor Southworth (Henry Jekyll/Edward Hyde), (back) Tori Rathbun (Emma Carew). Photo courtesy of Mike Kitaif.

Pages 90–91: *Coppelia,* Interlochen Arts Academy, Corson Hall, Interlochen, MI, December 2000. Choreographer Sharon Randolph, Scenic Design: Glen Vanderbilt, Costume Design: Candice Hughes.

Pages 92–93: *Willy Wonka Jr.,* Straz Center, Patel Conservatory, Ferguson Hall, August 2009. Director: Allison Burns, Scenic Design: Megan Byrne, Costume Design: Mary Rodriguez.

Page 94–95: *The Fantasticks,* Hat Trick Theatre Company, Tampa, FL, April 2010. Director: Joe Winskye, Scenic Design: Ian Mills, Costume Design: Kami Jacobs.

Pages 96–97: *Jesus Christ Superstar,* University of Northern Colorado, Langworthy Theatre, Greeley, CO, February 2018. Director: David Grapes, Scenic Design: J. David Blatt, Costume Design: Anne Toewe+. Actors depicted: (kneeling) Cody Mowrey (Judas Iscariot), (standing) Michael Travis Risner (Caiaphas). Photo courtesy of David Grapes.

Pages 98–99: *An American Dream,* Straz Center, Ferguson Hall, Tampa, FL, May 2009. Choreographer: Peter Stark, Scenic Design: Michael Chamoun, Costumes from Orlando Ballet School.

Page 101: *Turandot,* Opera Tampa, Straz Center, Carol Morsani Hall, Tampa, FL, April 2004. Director: Vernon Hartmann, Scenic Design: Peter Dean Beck, Costumes: Costume World.

Pages 102–103: *Tosca,* Palm Beach Opera, Kravis Center, Dreyfoos Hall, West Palm Beach, FL, March 2011. Director: Massimo Casparon, Scenery: Sarasota Opera, Costumes: Malabar.

Pages 104–105: *A Doll's House,* American Stage Theatre Company, St. Petersburg, FL, November 2012. Artistic Director: Todd Olson, Director: Seth Gordon, Scenic Design: Jill Davis, Costume Design: Frank Chavez.

Pages 106–107: *Dear World,* Players Centre for the Performing Arts, Sarasota, FL, January 2012. Artistic Director: Jeffery Kin, Director: Michael Newton-Brown, Scenic Design, Michael Newton-Brown, Costume Design, Dee Richards.

Pages 108–109: *Aida,* Manatee Players, Riverfront Theatre, Bradenton, FL, February 2012. Director: Rick Kerby, Scenic Design: Marc Lalosh, Costume Design: Emilie Patterson. Actors depicted: (left) Trina Rizzo (Amneris), (center) Candace Delancy (Aida), (right) Billy Masuck (Radames).

Page 111: *Aida,* Lakeland Community Theatre, Lakeland, FL, July 2013. Artistic Director/Director/Scenic Design: Alan Reynolds+. Costume Design: Camille McClellan.

Page 113: *Singin' in the Rain,* Athens Theatre, DeLand, FL, April 2019. Artistic Director: Craig Uppercue, Directors: A. J. Garcia and C. J. Sikorski, Scenic Design: Craig Uppercue, Costume Design: Tamara Marke-Lares. Actor depicted: Nate Elliott (Don Lockwood). Photo courtesy of Mike Kitaif.

Pages 114–115: *Tarzan,* Manatee Performing Arts Center, Bradenton, FL, August 2014. Artistic Director/Director: Rick Kerby, Scenic Design: Dan Yerman, Costume Design: Becky Evans. Actors depicted: (left) Maverick Wolf (Young Tarzan), (right) MaryKate D. Glidewell (Kala).

Page 117: *Cabaret,* Theatre Winter Haven, Winter Haven, FL, July 1999. Producer: Norm Small, Director: Thom Altman, Scenic Design: Jim Beck, Costume Design: Camille McClellan.

Pages 118–119: *Roméo et Juliette (Opera),* Opera Tampa, Straz Center, Carol Morsani Hall, Tampa FL, December 2006. Director: David Lefkowich, Scenic Design: Peter Dean Beck, Costumes: Utah Opera. Photo courtesy of Opera Tampa/Straz Center.

Pages 120–121: *Into the Woods,* Orlando Shakespeare Theater, Orlando, FL, September 2006. Artistic Director: Jim Helsinger, Director: Patrick Flick, Scenic Design: Bert Scott+, Costume Design: Rebecca Turk. Actor depicted: Thursday Farrar* (Witch). Photo courtesy of Rob Jones.

Pages 122–123: *Jekyll and Hyde,* Athens Theatre, DeLand, FL, September 2018. Artistic Director: Craig Uppercue, Director: Trevor Southworth, Scenic Design: Tori Oakes, Costume Design: Tamara Marke-Lares. Actors depicted: (left) Christopher deJongh (Bishop of Basingstoke), (right) Trevor Southworth (Henry Jekyll/Edward Hyde). Photo courtesy of Mike Kitaif.

Page 125: *The Secret Garden, Manatee Performing Arts Center, Bradenton, FL, September 2015. Artistic Director/ Director: Rick Kerby, Scenic Design: Kenneth Mooney, Costume Design: Becky Evans. Actors depicted: (left) Emma Devine (Mary Lennox), (right) Sarah Cassidy (Lily).*

Page 127: *Jekyll and Hyde,* Athens Theatre, DeLand, FL, September 2018. Artistic Director: Craig Uppercue, Director: Trevor Southworth, Scenic Design: Tori Oakes, Costume Design: Tamara Marke-Lares. Photo courtesy of Mike Kitaif.

Page 128: *Skeleton Crew,* American Stage Theatre Company, St. Petersburg, FL, January 2020. Artistic Director: Stephanie Gularte, Director: L. Peter Callender, Scenic Design: Steven K Mitchell, Costume Design: Jill Castle, Projection Design: Jerid Fox. Actor depicted: Enoch Armando King* (Reggie).

Page 129: *Casa Blue,* American Stage Theatre Company, St. Petersburg, FL, July 2007. Artistic Director/Director: Todd Olson, Scenic Design: Michael Newton-Brown, Costume Design: Frank Chavez. Actor depicted: Jen Anaya (Frida at 25 years old).

Page 131: *The Royale,* American Stage Theatre Company, St. Petersburg, FL, September 2017. Artistic Director: Stephanie Gularte, Director: Lisa Powers Tricomi, Scenic Design: Jerid Fox, Costume Design: Trish Kelley. Actors depicted: (left) Rokia Shearin (Nina), (right) Aygemang Clay* (Jay).

Page 133: *Willy Wonka Jr.,* Straz Center, Patel Conservatory, Ferguson Hall, August 2009. Director: Allison Burns, Scenic Design: Megan Byrne, Costume Design: Mary Rodriguez.

Pages 134-135: *Naming True,* Urbanite Theatre, Sarasota, FL, May 2017. Artistic Directors: Brendan Ragan/Summer Dawn Wallace, Director: Daniel Kelly, Scenic Design: Jeff Weber, Costume Design: Becki Leigh. Actor depicted: Minka Wiltz* (Nell). Photo courtesy of Dylan Jon Wade Cox.

Page 137: *Assassins,* Manatee Performing Arts Center, Bradenton, FL, October 2016. Artistic Director/Director: Rick Kerby, Scenic Design: Kenneth Mooney, Costume Design: Becky Evans.

Page 139: *Chess,* Manatee Performing Arts Center, Bradenton, FL, February 2016. Artistic Director/Director: Rick Kerby, Scenic Design: Kenneth Mooney.

Page 141: *Follies,* Players Centre for the Performing Arts, Sarasota, FL, March 2019. Artistic Director/Director: Jeffery Kin, Scenic Design: Ken Junkins, Costume Design: Georgina Wilmott. Photo courtesy of Ken Junkins.

Page 147 (Top): *The Royale,* American Stage Theatre Company, St. Petersburg, FL, September 2017. Artistic Director: Stephanie Gularte, Director: Lisa Powers Tricomi, Scenic Design: Jerid Fox, Costume Design: Trish Kelley, Actors depicted: L-R Kim Sullivan* (Wynton), Aygemang Clay* (Jay), Richard B. Watson*(Max), Rich Lowe (Fish), Rokia Shearin (Nina). Photo courtesy of American Stage Theatre Company.

Page 147 (Bottom Left): *The Royale,* American Stage Theatre Company, St. Petersburg, FL, September 2017. Artistic Director: Stephanie Gularte, Director: Lisa Powers Tricomi, Scenic Design: Jerid Fox, Costume Design: Trish Kelley. Actor depicted: Aygemang Clay* (Jay). Photo courtesy of American Stage Theatre Company.

Page 147 (Bottom Right): *The Royale,* Stage Theatre Company, St. Petersburg, FL, September 2017. Artistic Director: Stephanie Gularte, Director: Lisa Powers Tricomi, Scenic Design: Jerid Fox, Costume Design: Trish Kelley. Actors depicted: (left) Rokia Shearin (Nina), (right) Aygemang Clay* (Jay). Photo courtesy of American Stage Theatre Company.

Page 149: *Newsies,* Manatee Performing Arts Center, Bradenton, FL, July 2018. Artistic Director and Director: Rick Kerby, Scenic Design: Donna Buckalter, Costume Design: Matt Myers.

Pages 150–151: *Newsies,* Manatee Performing Arts Center, Bradenton, FL, July 2018. Artistic Director and Director: Rick Kerby, Scenic Design: Donna Buckalter, Costume Design: Matt Myers. Actors depicted: (left) Austin Gresham (Jack Kelly), (right) Cory L. Woomert (Joseph Pulitzer).

Pages 152–153: *American Buffalo,* Palm Beach Dramaworks, West Palm Beach, FL, November 2010. Scenic Design: Michael Amico.

Pages 154–155: *Lady Swanwhite,* Straz Center, Ferguson Hall, Tampa, FL, February 2019. Scenic Design: C.J. Marshall, Costume Design: Ann Jones. Photo by Will Staples, Courtesy of Opera Tampa/Straz Center for the Performing Arts.

Pages 156–157: *Lady Swanwhite,* Straz Center, Ferguson Hall, Tampa, FL, February 2019. Scenic Design: C.J. Marshall, Costume Design: Ann Jones. Photo courtesy of Kristin Coppola.

Page 161: *Doors,* Beacon Dance Festival, Palladium Theatre, St. Petersburg, FL, April 2019. Producer: Helen Hansen French. Dancers depicted: (left) Helen Hansen French, (right) Alex Jones. Photo courtesy of Tom Kramer.

Pages 162–163: *Nomadic Tempest,* Tall Ship *Amara Zee,* St. Petersburg, FL, April 2017. Director: Paul Kirby, Scenic/Costume Design: Adriana Kelder. Photo courtesy of Kristen Perry.

Pages 166–167: *Nomadic Tempest,* Tall Ship *Amara Zee,* St. Petersburg, FL, April 2017. Director: Paul Kirby, Scenic/Costume Design: Adriana Kelder. Photo courtesy of Kristen Perry.

Page 182: *Les Miserables,* Manatee Performing Arts Center, Bradenton, FL, August 2013. Artistic Director/Director: Rick Kerby, Scenic Design: Kirk V. Hughes, Costume Design: David Walker.

Back Cover: *Tarzan,* Manatee Performing Arts Center, Bradenton, FL, August 2014. Artistic Director/Director: Rick Kerby, Scenic Design: Dan Yerman, Costume Design: Becky Evans. Actors depicted: (left) Maverick Wolf (Young Tarzan), (right) MaryKate D. Glidewell (Kala).

* denotes member of Actors' Equity Association

+ denotes member of United Scenic Artist Local USA 829

Joseph P. Oshry

Designed Lighting LLC

941-518-5383

joseph@josephoshry.com

View Joseph Oshry's
profile on Linkedin   Follow Joseph Oshry
on Facebook

Bon Aventure!

Les Miserables, Manatee Performing Arts Center, Bradenton, FL, August 2013

Made in United States
North Haven, CT
11 September 2023

41418934R00106